CHEW MAGNA AND THE CHEW VALLEY

In *Chew Magna and the Chew Valley*, Ian and Mary Durham have brought together nearly 150 archive photographs and drawings to create a fascinating portrait of community life ranging back more than one hundred years.

To do so, they have drawn on the personal reminiscences, family albums and documents of many Chew residents. In these pages, we see familiar buildings in a variety of guises, as well as some which have now disappeared, historic events captured for posterity, local families and village characters, as well as men and women going about their daily work. In all, twelve sections encompass various aspects of village life, ranging from its houses, large and small, to life during two world wars.

The book is enhanced by many superb images from the camera of Charles Hutchins, local shopkeeper-cum-photographer, in the period 1895 to 1920. These were made possible by the lucky discovery of his original glass negatives, still in their original storage boxes.

By including a number of drawings by John Buckler, W. W. Wheatley and others, the authors have also been able to extend their pictorial survey to the early nineteenth century to show buildings and scenes from before the days of photography.

Added interest is provided by a selection of old photographs of the nearby villages of Bishop Sutton, Chew Stoke, Pensford, Stanton Drew, West Harptree and Winford.

THE AUTHORS

Ian and Mary Durham met at Oxford and married when Ian returned from service in the Far East in 1946. Ian was a Senior Lecturer in the Department of Extra-Mural Studies at Bristol University and for nearly twenty years served as a magistrate on the Bristol Bench. Mary for 23 years taught French at the Covent of the Sacred Heart High School, Chew Magna.

Both have long been interested in local history as a hobby. Ian Durham started the Forest of Dean Local History Society when they lived there, and Mary has been Secretary of the Chew Valley Local History Society since its formation in 1973. Together, they have given many illustrated talks and have a large collection of local history photographs and other material.

CHEW MAGNA

AND THE

CHEW VALLEY

Ian and Mary Durham

First published in 1991 by Redcliffe Press Ltd.,
49 Park St., Bristol

Reprinted January 1992 and September 1996

© Ian and Mary Durham

ISBN 1 872971 61 X

Typeset and printed by The Longdunn Press Ltd, Bristol

CONTENTS

PREFACE

Our collection of photographs and drawings of Chew Magna and the nearby villages started in 1977 when we undertook, as part of the Silver Jubilee celebrations, to organise an exhibition of local history material and to give a slide show on the history of the village.

For that event local residents produced many old photographs and documents, and allowed us to make copies. A very considerable stimulus came from the discovery of glass negatives of photographs taken by Mr. C.W. Hutchins, a local shopkeeper, in the period 1895 to 1920. These were in the possession of his daughter, Mrs. Doris Hobbs, still in the original storage boxes but, unfortunately, with little description of the subject matter. Their interpretation has been an intriguing exercise and many elderly local inhabitants, especially those who were brought up in the Chew Valley, have helped. Another set of glass negatives, almost as old as the Hutchins ones, are held by Mr. and Mrs. Maurice Hasell, who belong to a family settled in the area since medieval days.

To them and to all who have helped, by giving or lending photographs and by providing information, we are very grateful. Especially we would mention Geoffrey Hobbs, Sheila Walker, Arthur Young, Len Close, Ernest Hucker, Tim Bailey, Jim Cole, Jean Harding, Betty Arthur, Pat Gallop, Joe Peters, Jack Pearce, Tony Page, Sheila Weatherall, Harold Taviner, Rosalind Anstey, Jeanne and Hugh Moore, Allen and Jenny Griffin and for help with photography our thanks go to Peter Lloyd-Jones.

We have included a number of drawings done by John Buckler, W.W. Wheatley and others during the early part of last century. These enable us to go back even further to see how buildings and scenes appeared in the past, before the days of photography, and seem to serve the same purpose as the later photographs. There is a comprehensive collection of such drawings, covering most villages, in the care of David Bromwich, the Local History Librarian, at Taunton Castle. We thank him for his help.

The majority of the pictures in this collection relate to Chew Magna, but the middle part of the valley, the area round the lake, should be considered as an entity. So it seemed appropriate to include some old photographs of other local villages and hope they will be of interest both to residents and visitors.

INTRODUCTION

The River Chew flows for 17 miles through the rural countryside of south Avon, or, as many people would still prefer to say, the plain of north Somerset. From its origin as a spring at Chewton Mendip it flows north and joins the River Avon at Keynsham. Chew Magna is about half way along the river's course and it is the village offering shopping, commercial, professional and medical services to the residents of that part of the valley. Throughout the centuries, as the name implies, it has been the biggest of the villages along the river and in some ways the most important, not least when the Bishop of Bath and Wells was the Lord of the Manor and had one of his many palaces here. The remains of this are the present day Chew Court.

The proximity of the big port and commercial centre of Bristol, just over Dundry Hill, has caused the village to be, to some extent, a dormitory area. Richer merchants and professional people from the city have built bigger than average houses here and have made their own valuable contributions to village life. But planning controls have resulted in very little expansion of the village and little destruction of its historic heritage. The present village still has at its centre the medieval buildings and the narrow streets of the early village, and it is still surrounded by fertile countryside and fine old farmhouses.

The making of the Chew Valley Lake in the early 1950s has created a new situation, with additional facilities for sport and relaxation, and the area has taken on more the atmosphere of a tourist area. It welcomes and caters for an increasing number of visitors who come to enjoy the beauties of the Chew Valley and to appreciate its history.

THE CENTRE OF THE VILLAGE

Buckler's Drawing 1834 This drawing, entitled 'Church House at Chew Magna' was done by John Chessell Buckler and is in the Piggott Collection at Taunton Castle Museum. All the buildings still exist, some with new frontages, even the small building, which was a carpenter's workshop. That has been converted into a cottage now hidden by the bank. The Church House (now known as the Old Schoolroom) had more windows and doors than today. It housed the school upstairs and the workhouse downstairs. Note the mounting steps beside the inn sign.

Village Centre c.1880 The earliest known photograph of the village, taken before the Bear and Swan was altered in 1886 to give it two bay windows. The railings were already along the high pavement, a house called Prospect Villa and its garden occupied the site of the future hotel (now the Co-op), and the Old Bakehouse was a private house with a garden and trees. Mr. Urch's house on the extreme right was thatched and was probably two cottages. Note the horse drinking at the trough of the village pump, outside the shop.

The Old Toll House The Toll House stood in the middle of the road near the Triangle, at the junction of The Chalks and Tunbridge Road, and was not the building now occupied by the estate agency. The high pavement for pedestrians passed behind it. Note the gates for vehicles and for pedestrians on each road. A small carriage is shown parked on the left, just beyond the railings, probably one of those available for hire as transport to the railway station at Pensford. The Toll House was demolished about 1880.

South Parade and Prospect House Hotel This tranquil scene shows only horse-drawn vehicles in the village centre, about 1900. The three-storey Prospect House Hotel has replaced the house of that name and the lower part of it survives to the present as the Co-op. Note the lamp standards on the pavement, possible only because the village had its own gas works from about 1868 until after the nationalisation of gas.

Chew Magna Street

Village Centre, looking East, c.1915 The house which was later to accommodate the first bank in the village was erected in 1852 between the Old Schoolroom and the Saddlers. The latter was the Baptist Chapel from 1829 to 1844, which would account for its appearance and for the tank, with steps leading down into it, which was found under the floor of the front room. The figure of the white horse, an indication that the saddler's craft was carried on here, can be seen in the shop window. By this time the extension had been built in front of the hardware shop, on the left, and was accommodating the cobbler. The records of the Pelican Inn, on the right, go back to 1615. The car is a Renault of Edwardian vintage.

'Bank' House This house was built in 1852 and later provided accommodation for the first bank in the village, Parr's Bank, later the Westminster Bank. In 1916 the bank moved to the downstairs front room of the Old Schoolroom next door, at a rent of £5 per annum. The house had a tunnel under the house, visible above the car, to allow the owner to take his horse and trap through to the garden behind. The house was demolished in the 1930s when the present bank was built. The car is of the type generally known as a 'bull-nosed' Morris.

Corner Shop and The Chalks This photograph, taken from the spot where the Toll House once stood, shows front doors from several cottages opening onto this narrow road. Some houses have been demolished but the road retains its medieval width. The Chalks probably gets its name from Sir Richard Chokke, Lord Chief Justice of Common Pleas in London and Lord of the Manor of Stanton Drew in the 15th century. The railings, of an unusual pattern, are said to have been made at the Evans foundry at Paulton, probably during the last century.

12

South Parade, Chew Magna.

8075

South Parade, c.1915 The Miltons, father and son, were chemists and stationers, and ran the Post Office from about 1883 to 1926, when William Milton died. Like his father he was the local Registrar of births and deaths. This photograph shows the staff outside the shop. The range of transport is interesting.

Prospect Cottage and Harford Square Prospect Cottage, on the left, was occupied by Mr. and Mrs. Spear. He was the blacksmith and together they were responsible for the village telephone exchange in the cottage next door. He also looked after the public weighbridge out in the square. The cottages were demolished in 1966 when the Midland Bank was built. Harford Square, like Harford House in the centre background, was named after the family which lived in the Manor House from 1798 to 1844.

Silver Street and foundations for the Church Hall, 1923 These cottages in Silver Street, stretching in a long row down to the bridge, were demolished in 1963 to provide a site for Stoneleigh and other modern houses. The stone for the Church Hall came from a quarry in Hanny's Lane, just across Norton Lane. At one time there were more cottages on the churchyard side of Silver Street. The only one remaining is generally called the Sexton's Cottage but he has not lived there since about 1945.

GENERAL VIEW OF CHEW MAGNA FROM THE BATCH.

View from The Batch, with the Seven Bells This general view of the village shows several features which have disappeared. The nearest group of houses was known as the Seven Bells, supposedly because at one time the tenants made up the team of bellringers at the parish church. They were demolished when the council houses were built on the site in the 1920s. Just visible, to the right of the church tower is the Sexton's Cottage which still remains in Silver Street and, to the left of it, the ruins of the houses adjoining, which disappeared early this century.

CHURCH AND CHAPEL

Church of St. Andrew c.1900 There were many trees in the churchyard. The church was built in the 13th–15th centuries, to replace an earlier, probably wooden one, which was mentioned in documents in 1191. Its size reflects the fact that it was a 'minster' church, with the clergy having responsibility for surrounding parishes and the people of those parishes being responsible, until relatively recent times, for the upkeep of the walls and gates round the churchyard at Chew Magna. The tower is one of the famous 'Somerset' type and there has been a clock in the tower since the early 1700s.

The de Hauteville Effigy The famous wooden effigy in the south aisle is late medieval but the canopy above and the name underneath are not, as is shown by this drawing made by Buckler in 1834. At that time the statue was on the window ledge in the Baber Chapel. It probably represents John Wyck, a latter owner of Norton Manor, who died in 1346. The last of the de Hautevilles died long before that kind of armour was worn.

Bells after removal from the church tower 1898 The original bells were re-cast by the celebrated Thomas Bilbie of Chew Stoke in 1735 to make a peal of six and in 1898, to celebrate the Diamond Jubilee of Queen Victoria, two of these were re-cast and two repaired. Here we have, from left to right, the boy Veater, Mr. J. Evans, Dr. Collins, Mr. Colston (Churchwarden), Mr. C.W. Hutchins and the Verger, Benjamin Gover with the bells removed from the tower. The old Vicarage is in the background.

Bells on carts en route for London The bells are on the carts outside the Bear and Swan before starting the journey to the Whitechapel foundry in London. After these six were re-hung another two bells were added in 1928 to complete the octave, which still includes two Bilbie bells.

The Tenor Bell This shows the tenor bell ready to be hoisted back into the belfry in 1899. It carries a likeness of Queen Victoria and the inscription 'To the Glory of God and to commemorate the Diamond Jubilee of Her Most Gracious Majesty Queen Victoria, Queen of Great Britain and Ireland and Empress of India. God Save the Queen'. Standing beside the bell is the Verger, Benjamin Gover who died the night before the bells were rededicated, a few days after this photograph was taken. At 82 he was said to be the oldest sexton in the country and he held the office for fifty seven years.

Baptist Chapel Conference 1912 Mr. Hutchins, the village photographer, was a great supporter of the Baptist Chapel and he recorded this group at the Baptist Itinerant Society conference, held in Chew Magna. The ladies in the front row were local and catered for the event, the gentlemen behind were the preachers who visited the villages around Bristol to take the services.

THE OLD SCHOOLROOM

Manor House at Chew Magna.

Drawing from Rutter's 'Delineations' 1829 This drawing shows the Church House, later known as the Old Schoolroom, with more windows and doors on the south side that at present. From the mid 1600s a school was accommodated upstairs and the village poor house was down below, where the large room was divided into cubicles, each of which housed a family or a destitute person. Rutter calls this the Manor House because it was still the legal meeting place of the Courts Leet and Baron of the Lord of the Manor. The announcement of 'Obediah York's Commercial Academy' above the door shows that another, rather unusual, educational activity was also being conducted there.

Old Schoolroom and Blind House 1848 This drawing is by W.W. Wheatley and is in the Braikenridge Collection. 'Blind house' is usually a euphemism for 'lock-up' and there are references in the Vestry Books to prisoners being kept here overnight before being taken before the magistrates. The building through the archway on the left was a house in the churchyard, owned by the parish and let out to pauper families. It was demolished in 1865.

Exterior of Old Schoolroom, c.1910 For many years there was a small area, enclosed by a low wall and iron railings, in front of the Old Schoolroom. The railings went as scrap in the 1939–45 War and the area was levelled and paved in 1983. According to Frederick Wood, writing in 1903, the date 1510 was visible at that time above the front door and that would indicate the age of the building.

Interior, upstairs, 1965 This shows the upstairs room as it was when the building was closed as unsafe in 1965. Features which disappeared in the repairs were the round window in the end wall (that was inserted last century to give more light to the schoolroom), the ceiling which hid much of the original wooden roof, and the fireplaces, the only means of heating the school. This photograph shows the platform and piano which helped to make this hall the centre of village social life.

Interior, downstairs, 1960. The lower room was rented by the Men's Club until 1965 and was equipped with two full sized billiard tables. These were not appreciated by the Youth Club for whom the building was re-opened in 1971 and were sold.

During major repairs and alterations, 1971 This shows how extensive were the 1971 repairs. The massive oak beams supporting most of the upper floor had to be replaced and the fine original timber roof was strengthened and preserved. The building became an Area Youth Club for nine years but was then purchased by the Parish Council. In 1981 it became the Village Hall.

HOUSES: LARGE AND SMALL

Chew Court early in the 19th century In the fourteenth century the Bishop of Bath and Wells built a palace or manor house next to the church in Chew Magna, and a little survives in the present Chew Court. The gatehouse with its turrets and the wall adjoining are part of the original house, which was probably built round a quadrangle. In 1834, when this drawing was made by Buckler, the Court was occupied by a small farmer who used the 14th century gatehouse as a barn. The water shown in the foreground suggests that there may once have been a moat.

Chew Court early in the 20th century Restored as a 'gentleman's' residence, and with gardeners and other staff, the Court is covered with Virginia Creeper. The gatehouse and the lower part of the adjoining wing are part of the original Bishop's palace.

The Manor House – A drawing of 1868 The other quite big house is at the far end of the village from Chew Court. Its Gothic exterior, dating only from 1874, encloses the remains of a Tudor house. One feature, a round tower called the Henry VII tower, may be even older. William Penn preached here in 1687 and from 1680 to 1844 it was the home of prominent Quaker families, the Vickris, the Summers and the Harfords.

The Manor House – Interior in the 1930s Before 1939 this was a miniature stately home, with panelling and fine fireplaces, period furniture and even a priest's hole. Although the army requisitioned the building in 1940 they abandoned it when they discovered that it had no running water, modern sanitation or electricity. The house was then bought by the Sisters of the Order of Our Lady of the Missions, who evacuated their convent school from Deal to Chew Magna. The senior school was closed in 1986 but a junior school continues in modern buildings in the grounds. The Manor House, a listed building, awaits a new use.

The Old Vicarage This Victorian vicarage, built in the time of the Rev. A.E. Ommanney, replaced an older building nearer the church and rarely used as a home by the vicars. What was suitable for Mr. Ommanney with his ten children and numerous staff has proved an embarrassment to later incumbents and it was abandoned as a vicarage in 1987. It is now divided into two residences, one half being called Prospect House. The picture shows the Rev. John Galbraith, Vicar from 1878 to 1916.

Longchalks (Mapstone's Cottage) This photograph, entitled 'Mapstone's Cottage' in the Wood Collection at Weston-super-Mare, is the house now called Longchalks on the Pensford road out of the village. It has been the police station, butcher's shop (with slaughter house in the adjoining yard) and the home of the fly proprietor who ran the service to Bristol and to Pensford station. It was originally two cottages and was thatched until the 1930s.

Dower Cottage (Breddisholme) Called Breddisholme when this photograph was taken, it was the home in his retirement of Dr. Collins and his daughter. The name was changed when the widow of Dr. Brew (Senior) went to live there.

Manor Cottage This little cottage, in the bottleneck on the Winford road, has now been trebled in size and is approached from behind, via the car park. The lady is Mrs. Bailey, with her son William.

Fisher's Lodge Certainly built before 1824, this has been the home of Mr. Dowling, who owned the coal mines at Bishop Sutton, and Mr. Nicholls and Mr. Atchley, solicitors. This is Mr. Atchley in about 1910. The house is now divided, the rear part retaining the name and the front half being called Archways.

Houses at the top of High Street These two houses stood at the top of High Street, on what is now the car park adjoining the Roman Catholic Church. They were demolished early this century.

SHOPS AND OTHER BUILDINGS

Prospect House Hotel Built at the end of last century, the lower two floors still survive as the Co-op. Stores. The upper two storeys constituted the hotel, offering tea, coffee and dining rooms, while part of the ground floor was occupied by 'Sunny Jim', the barber, open 8 a.m. to 8 p.m., with haircuts costing sixpence. The verandah was removed about 1920 and the top storey in the early 1960s. The cottage to the right of the hotel was the local telephone exchange. It was demolished in 1966, to be replaced by the Midland Bank.

Mr. Hutchins' Shop This was the home and shop of the local photographer, Charles William Hutchins. It was a draper's shop but with sidelines such as the paraffin lamps which can be seen in the windows. So Mrs. Fitzgerald carries on an old tradition in the same shop today. The greenhouse was replaced by another small shop which became the cobbler's and is now the hardware section. The cottage on the other side lost its garden and became Barclays Bank, which closed in 1990.

Miss Hutchins' Shop and the Parish Pump The Pantry of today as it appeared in 1905, when this shop was run by the sister of the photographer. It had been acquired by their parents in 1867. Note the servant girls just inside the door, and the pump, with its trough, outside. This pump was the main source of water in the village but many houses had their own pumps or wells. There was much controversy as to whether the water was pure and safe. The doctors said it was not, but a public meeting in 1907 decided against the expense of a piped supply. That was not installed in the village until 1937.

The interior of Miss Hutchins' shop A wide range of goods was offered for sale, which required three different sets of scales. More valuable unpacked items were kept in the small drawers and canisters behind the counter. There was no self-service and chairs were provided so that ladies could sit while giving their orders.

The enlarged shop and new parish pump By the time of the First World War the grocery shop had been extended by a new wing and the village had a new pump, with the handle pointing the other way. This pump was only removed in 1962 and found a home in the garden of Harford House. The well from which the water was taken still exists, covered by a metal plate just outside the present shop door. The photograph shows Miss Weaver, who was then managing the shop, and Mr. Coates.

The Corner Shop Now the estate agents, this was once a blacksmith's, later a tobacconist's and sweet shop, but never the toll house. Note the cottage further along Tunbridge Road, probably dating from the 17th century, which was restored to become Wellington Galleries and then became an extension of the estate agency.

Staddlestones This house, the new Vicarage since 1987, was originally two cottages, built probably in the 16th century. The date stone on the front, inscribed 'AEK 1697' is thought to indicate the date of a major rebuilding. For much of the last hundred years it has been a butcher's shop, well remembered for its canopy and the strange figure of a helmetted female above the shop-window. The picture shows Mrs. Goodland, wife of the butcher who occupied the house and shop before it was taken over by Jack Pearce's father, Clifford, in 1932. In 1960 the business was moved to the other shop at the bottom of the High Street.

After the Fat Stock Show Before Christmas the carcasses of prize-winning cattle were exhibited in front of the shop. The picture shows Job Goodland with his sons Tom and Reginald.

39

Tunbridge Mill Almost certainly on the site of one of the mills mentioned in the Domesday Survey, the undershot water wheel survives, but in poor condition. The mill was involved in the storage and distribution of animal foods and agricultural commodities until 1991.

Gas Works from the Silver Street Bridge The gas works operated from about 1865 to 1955. It consisted of a retort house and five retorts, a purifier house, meter house, gasometer and fuel store. There was also a manager's house. After gas nationalisation in 1947 this works was closed and gas was brought by pipe over Dundry hill.

Mr. Sparkes, Manager of the Gas Works It was called the 'one man gas works'. After the original company went bankrupt in 1921 the works was auctioned and was bought by a farmer, Wallington Brimble of Round House Farm, who put in his son-in-law, Herbert Sparkes, to run the show. He said 'I used to do the lot, run the works, get the coal, put in meters and stoves, lay the mains and so on.'

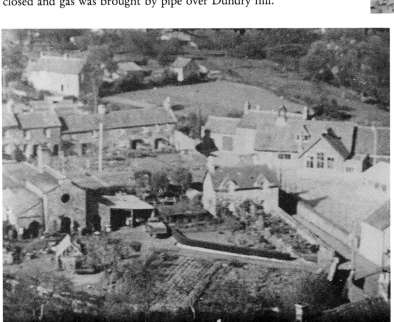

Gas Works from the Church Tower This 1930s view from the church tower shows the gas works on the left, with Gas Crescent behind and, in the background, Elm Farm. The school is on the right. The manager's house, between works and school, has survived but the rest of the site was cleared in 1970 and the Streamside estate built there.

FAMILY GROUPS AND VILLAGE PERSONALITIES

The Hutchins Family, c.1904 This is the family which late last century and early in this one provided many of the shopping facilities in the village. Mrs. Anna Hutchins, on the right in the middle row, is the widow of Charles James Hutchins who took over from the Seviers at the baker's and grocer's shop (now The Pantry) in 1867. In the back row are her children William, Charles and Amy, and beside her are her daughters-in-law. The children are Dorothy Jones and Doris Hutchins (later Mrs. Hobbs). Charles was the photographer who left an excellent record of village life in photographs taken between 1895 and 1920. Thirty of them are reproduced in this collection. He had the draper's shop (now Mrs. Fitzgerald's) in South Parade and he built Chew Hill House.

The Family of Sylvester Williams in 1903 Sylvester Williams was descended from Obediah York who ran the Commercial Academy in the Old Schoolroom and who lived in the Toll House. He was a gardener at the Manor House and had this family of six sons and three daughters. Mrs. Annie Gunter, who died in 1990 aged 90 years, is the youngest child on her father's knee.

Annie Gunter The youngest child of Sylvester Williams, she went back to live in the family home, Brook Cottage, when her father died in 1924 and lived there for a further sixty-seven years. In 1984 Annie Gunter published her life story, *Treasured Memories.* The photograph shows Brook Cottage.

The Lovern Family at Church House This shows Edith and Walter Lovern with some of their family at the time of the Coronation in 1937, outside Church House in Silver Street. This was the family home from 1900 to 1967. Walter was a high class tailor, patronised by the local gentry and farmers, and employed several assistants who worked in the traditional way, sitting crosslegged on the floor. He was a Methodist Lay Preacher, Secretary of the Gas Works company and a member of the Parish Council for many years. The boy on the extreme left is David Walker, a grandson of Walter Lovern.

Mr. Gallop and Granddaughter On a tombstone in the churchyard, with the cross and the Old Schoolroom in the background, sits John Gallop with little Emily Gallop, his granddaughter. He was then 80 years old and lived in the cottage behind the bank. Emily later married Mr. Percy Gallop and so retained her name, and shortly before she died in 1988 she recalled the occasion of the photograph. Her grandfather had met her in the churchyard, and the photographer, Mr. Hutchins, ever watchful for a good picture, just happened to be near. Mr. Gallop was known to have walked to Ashton Court, and back again, to do a day's work. He died in 1918, aged 91.

Albert Gallop with Serpent A son of John Gallop, Albert was an outstanding member of a family renowned for their interest in music and their support for the Methodist Chapel. He played the piano, trumpet, concertina and tuba, and he conducted the Salvation Army band. He also played this unusual instrument, a serpent, in the Chew Stoke band and later donated it to the Bristol Museum.

Mr. and Mrs. Adlam They lived at the Manor House from 1864 to 1903 and completely changed it to give the present Gothic appearance. This photograph is from a periodical *The Animal's Friend* which describes how Mr. and Mrs. Adlam were the inspiration for the setting up of 'The International Association for the Total Suppression of Vivisection' in 1876.

Mr. Frederick Wood A local solicitor and renowned antiquarian, he lived at Highfields and in 1903 published *Collections for a Parochial History of Chew Magna*, a most valuable source of material on local and family history. He and his staff copied records like the parish registers and vestry minutes, and deposited them in the public library at Weston-super-Mare, which library had been established with the help of a large donation from Mr. Wood.

Mr. and Mrs. Stampe Eugene Stampe was the village schoolmaster from 1875 until he retired in 1915. He married Mary King, eldest daughter of Frederick King the wheelwright, and they lived at The Sycamores in the High Street. He died aged 88 years in 1938, having spent almost all his working life in the village and after playing a very active part, often as secretary, in many village organisations. He was a great church worker and was choirmaster for sixteen years. This is their Golden Wedding photograph, when the village gave them fifty golden sovereigns.

The Snail Man Known as Nommy Nupple, or the Snail Man, he wandered round local villages for many years, poking the snails out of the stone walls and collecting them in his can. It was said he sold them to the gourmet restaurants in Bristol. He lived rough, sleeping in outhouses and barns and died about 1942.

Charlie Hall and Rene Sage Here seen together at the 1977 Local History Exhibition are two highly respected old residents, both now dead. Charlie Hall was born in the Seven Bells, left school at 13 to work on a farm for four shillings a week but then went to help his father digging drains. He served in Gallipoli during the war and returned to be a coal miner until 1932, when he became licensee of the Queen's Arms. He was Sexton for forty years and captain of the bell ringers. He died in 1985, aged 91. Rene Sage was born in the village, a lively and outspoken personality. One of a large family, poverty in childhood shaped her politics and she was a founder member of the Chew Magna Labour Party. She always took great interest in village affairs.

CHILDREN AND SCHOOL

The Tea Party A happy occasion of make-believe. The 'hostess' is Doris, daughter of the photographer, Charles Hutchins.

Children's dress in the early 20th century One for the family album. Mr. Hutchins photographed many local children.

The Hutchins boys playing Solitaire Mr. Hutchins' photograph of his two sons is a very successful interior study, at a time when a long exposure was necessary and any movement spoilt the picture. Richard, nearer the camera, was drowned in the 1914–18 war and the entry on the war memorial in St. Andrew's Church, '2nd. Officer Richard L. Hutchings. H.M.T. Trinidad' is one of those rare instances of a spelling mistake on a cenotaph.

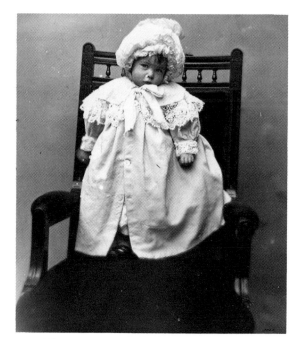

The youngest sitter A very young customer.

School Class in 1904 This class at the recently built Chew Magna School shows a wide age range and contains Norman Douglas Walker (third from right, back row) and his future wife, Norah Lovern (third from left, second row) as well as Howard Lovern (extreme right, second row) who was for many years the Correspondent of the school.

Mr. Stampe and his Staff Perhaps this was something of a re-union because the staff of the village school was rarely more than the headmaster and one teacher. Possibly it was the occasion of the retirement of Mr. Stampe, Headmaster from 1875 to 1915. In the front row are Mr. Stampe and Mrs. K. Walker, behind are Miss G. Stampe, Miss Thomas, Mrs. Hamblin and Miss Amy Chick.

SOCIETIES AND CLUBS

Druids' Parade 1895 The procession has formed outside the Bear and Swan. The officers dressed appropriately and were mounted; some wore sashes. The 'club' days were often holidays for all in the village, with many children absent from the school if it did remain open. The Druids' banner was taken into safe keeping at Bristol when the local branch was wound up in 1977.

Druids' Parade 1905 This later parade is outside the Pelican and again there are horsemen and officers wearing sashes, and the banner. But the gathering is largely of boys of school age. In addition to the Druids there were branches of the Oddfellows and the Buffaloes in the village. In return for a small weekly subscription these friendly societies provided sickness and unemployment benefit and paid for the burial of members and their families.

Girls' Training Corps, c.1952 This organisation was created during the 1939–45 war and seems to have largely replaced the Girl Guides locally. Even the leader, Mrs. Hughes, switched her allegiance. Others taking a leading part included Mrs. Clifford-Smith, Mrs. Betty Crocker, Pat Stevens (later Mrs. Coles), Lena Price (Mrs. Church), Betty England (Mrs. Backhuys) and Pat Gallop. The Chew Valley company was formed in 1942 and wound up in 1965. There is a seat in the churchyard given by the girls in memory of Dr. and Mrs. Hughes.

Girls' Training Corps, Drama Rehearsal Parades were held weekly and activities included marching and drill, first aid, handicrafts (especially woodwork), public speaking and drama. This company won the national award for the best Coronation Album in 1953 and won the county championship for drama in 1948 with their production of 'Player Queen'. Their producer was Dr. Hughes, seen here with (left to right) Gertie Hayman, Edith Bryant, Sheila Perry, Kathleen Smart, Sylvia George, Sheila Harris, Lena Price, and (sitting) Hazel Hodge and Edna Ward.

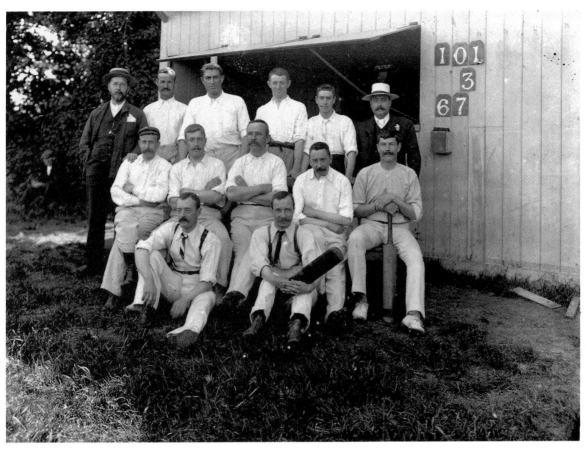

Cricket Team, c.1912 There has been a Chew Magna Cricket Club for almost a hundred years. This one must be of about 1912 and the names of players were: Mr. Milton (Postmaster), Jack Trendall, Albert Marsh, Victor England and two unknowns in the back row, Reg Goodland, Albert Woolard, Bill Webb, Mr. Atchley, Bradlaugh Peters and, in the front, Edward Colston and Walter Lovern.

Football Team, c.1910 This local football team includes in the back row, George Rook, Harry Edgell, — Perry, Bill Webb, Harry Peters, and Ben Faux; centre row, George Bates, Maurice(?) Veater, Bill Harris and, in the front, — Clark, Bill Emery, — Perry, — Rawlings, and Bill Brown.

Tug-of-War Team c.1930 Another form of competition between the villages was Tug-of-War, and this sport demanded consistent and serious training. This team practised by pulling against a tree in the orchard where Lower Batch is now. Names are, back row, from the left Ray Bell, Gerry Patch, unknown, Fred Clarke, Sam Moger, Samuel Taylor, Bill Iles, (?)Cyril Veater, Jim Bell and Albert Foote. Front row Unknown, Gilbert Marsh, Reg Pearce, Gilbert Sampson, Ted Hall and two unknowns.

EVENTS

Empire Day, c.1905 The children from the school, in their 'Sunday best', with teachers and helpers on Empire Day. They are outside the Pelican, ready to process through the village on their way to tea and games at one of the big houses.

Sunday Entertainment c.1905 Probably on Sunday, because the shops are closed, a travelling player with his monkey attracts the attention of the children. Some children were fetching water from the village pump in front of the shop. The boy in the school cap is William Hutchins and the older girl is Hoppy Dimond, so called because she was lame. Note the bare metal of the wheels of the pram holding the latest addition to the Dimond family. The spinal carriage was in common use for back sufferers.

Men's Outing This charabanc trip must have been in about 1925. The photograph would be taken at Gough's Cave, Cheddar and the names of the trippers are, back row, Albert Hobbs, Wallie Faux, unknown, Herbert Hobbs. Front row, George Chappell, Laurence Hobbs, Victor England, Harry Foote, driver unknown and Charlie Sage.

Ladies' Outing This may have been a little earlier than the men's outing but it was certainly less comfortable. Note the solid tyres of the charabanc. This excursion was probably organised by the local Women's Institute which had been started in 1917 by Mrs. Brew.

A Society Wedding This is almost certainly a wedding in the Colston family and is of interest because of the early century fashions.

The Rabbit Shoot In the days long before myxomatosis a day's shooting provided a good bag and a social occasion.

Bringing in the Harvest In a farming community there was no more important day than when the last of the crops was brought in from the fields. Family and friends, indoor staff as well as farm workers, joined in the final stages and in the Harvest Home to follow. This gathering was near Fisher's Lodge, very early this century.

Planting the Jubilee Tree, 1935 To mark the Silver Jubilee of King George the Fifth a tree was planted on the Triangle by Miss Beryl Mapstone, who was twenty-five years old on that day. The tree did not survive for long. All the trees and bushes were cleared when the low stone wall was built round the Triangle and it is another tree, planted after the Queen's visit in 1956, which flourishes there today.

Jubilee Procession, 1935: the Village Queen On this occasion there was a long procession, with a large proportion of the inhabitants taking part, and in fancy dress. Gwen Grey was the elected Queen and the attendants were Kathy Hall, Betty Arthur and Margaret Smith.

A Rival Village Queen For the same occasion Dennis Spear decided that his sister should also be queen. With the help of neighbour Mr. Hiscock, carpenter and undertaker, he made a suitable coach which he pulled himself. On the left are Dennis's parents and on the right Mr. and Mrs. Hiscocks. Dennis Spear has published a small book, *A Decade to Remember, Chew Magna 1930–1940* about his childhood memories.

The Druids in 1935 Probably the last time the Druids Friendly Society banner was paraded before it was taken to Bristol for safe keeping. The patrol leader scout who helped carry the banner is Allen Griffin. Others to be recognised are Mr. Davy, Arthur Spear, Wilf(?) Mapstone, Gordon Pickford and Arthur Lane. Those behind the beards cannot be identified.

Village Gathering on V.E. Day The photograph is taken from Harford House with Glebe House in the background. On the right are the two cottages, one of which housed the telephone exchange, which were demolished to provide the site for the Midland Bank. The hut was in connection with the public weighbridge. On the hut is a notice 'Air Raid Shelters' and an arrow pointing to the cellars of Harford House. The 30 m.p.h. speed limit applied only to the very centre of the village. The gathering is predominantly female or oldish men because the younger men have not yet returned. Children in the front are in patriotic fancy dress and there is a Cadet Corps band at the back. A few adults are in Air Raid Warden or Special Constable uniforms.

Queen Elizabeth II in Chew Magna In 1956 the Queen inaugurated the Chew Valley Lake reservoir and on her way to the ceremony she drove through the village. Here she is passing the Triangle and a large crowd was assembled to cheer. The village was decorated with flags and large decorated arches across the road at both ends of the village.

The Maypole on the Triangle A maypole on this spot had to be taken down in 1754 because it was unsafe. The tradition was revived for the Queen's visit in 1956 and to commemorate the occasion the cotoneaster tree was planted on the Triangle.

Queen Elizabeth II inaugurates Chew Valley Lake Queen Elizabeth with the Duke of Edinburgh and Mr. F.G. Robinson at the Commemoration Stone at the Chew Valley Lake on the 17th July 1956. The lake has added a very interesting feature to a beautiful valley and has made possible fishing, sailing and lakeside walks.

The Fire Engine The fire engine is of interest to young and old, especially when it gleams as this one did. There was a 'maintained' fire brigade in Chew Magna during the 1939–45 war, with a fire station at the western end of the present Co-op. building. It was disbanded in 1948 but re-formed when the new fire station was built in 1953. The picture is also of interest because it shows so well the top storey of the Co-op building and the cottages next to the Co-op, all of which were demolished in the 1960s.

THE WARS

Roll of Honour 1916 During the 1914–18 World War, as the men of the village enlisted, their names were written up on these boards outside the cobbler's shop, next to Mr. Hutchins. Only a few of those here recorded are still alive today. Mr. Hutchins is printing the name, watched by Mr. Stampe, the schoolmaster, and Mr. Atkins the cobbler.

Ladies' War Effort This was part of the campaign for self-sufficiency during the First World War. The Women's Institute organised classes where an instructor, the gentleman, taught ladies how to make their own baskets. The ladies are, from the left, Mrs. H. Atchley, Mrs. M. Hobbs, Mrs. E. Griffin, unknown and Miss Walker.

Returned from the First World War This photograph was taken in the yard behind the Bear and Swan and the occasion was to welcome the returning servicemen. Not all could attend but the group includes two of the doctors in the village.

Medals for the First World War To each of the returning ex-servicemen the village presented one of these medals, inscribed with the recipient's name. This one was presented to Victor Liddiatt.

77

1939 – 1945

This Scroll records the thanks of
The People of Chew Magna

to *N.º F. Veater. M.C.*
1st Northamptonshire Reg.t

for his service to his King and
Country in the cause of Freedom.

"HE the man who still with steadfast
heart strove for his country, who in
perilous days spared neither life nor
fortune, and bestowed most help when
most she needed."

Accius
Circa 150 B.C.

Certificates for the Second World War After the 1939–45 War the village gave this certificate to each of its ex-servicemen. Major Veater won his Military Cross in Burma, for consistent bravery during the crossing of the Irrawaddy and the recapture of Mandalay in February 1945.

Left panel (served):
Pte Thos Balch, R.F.A.
Pte Hy Davey, The Gloucesters
Pte Alf. J. Dimond, M.G.C.
Pte Alb E. Dimond, Royal Gloucester Hussars Yeomanry
Pte Percy Fry, R.G.A.
Pte Thos Harrison, R.A.F.
Pte Rbt Hawkins, Dorset Light Inf.
Pte Art. Hillier, R.I.R.
Pte Harry Hollister, Somerset Light Inf.
Pte Alb T. Marsh, R.F.A.
Pte Ern Mason, The Gloucesters
Gnr Alf Osborne, R.G.A.

Right panel (served):
Pte Wm. J. Parsons, R.A.S.C.
Pte Geo Parsons, M.R.P.
Pte Hy Pickford, Dorset Regt.
Sgn John G. Reeve, R.E.A.
Gnr John Sage, Royal R.G.A.
Sgt F.H. Stallard, 4th Yeoman Regt.
Pte Clifford T. Tripp, The Dorset Corps
Dvr John H. Vowles, R.F.A.
Pte Hy. Weaver, The London Corps
Pte Wm F. Wolfrake, R.G.L.I.
Pte Wm. Wilkins, R.F.C.
A. York

Central panel:
WINFORD IRON ORE & REDDING COY
In Gratefull Memory of those who
Served their King & Country in the
Great War. 1914-1918.

KILLED IN ACTION
ALBERT E. DIMOND
HARRY HOLLISTER
JOHN SAGE

Memorial for the Men of the Red Ochre Works On display at the small museum relating to the Red Ochre works, at the Winford Road Garage, is this triptych which lists the names of the men from the works who served in the 1914–18 war and, at the bottom of the central section, the names of those who died.

Local Home Guard Platoon This local platoon of the Home Guard in the 1939–45 war was part of the Second Somerset (Long Ashton) Home Guard Battalion. It was responsible for an area from the Bristol boundary to Priddy, and from Felton to the A37. The Officer Commanding was Major Frederick Terrell (of The Portugals) and the 2nd i/c was Captain Alexander Scott, M.C. (of The Rookery), both Chew Magna. The platoon commander, on the left of the photograph, was Richard Ryder who farmed Chew Court farm and was the local representative of the Ministry of Agriculture. He is remembered for long service as District Councillor, Chairman of Parish Council and Chairman of local charities.

OCCUPATIONS

The Staff at the Grange c.1910 These were the staff of Dr. and Mrs. Shaw at The Grange. Note the fine embroidery worn by the girls. The man on the left is Charlie Bell, the coachman, and the other is Ted Emery, the groom.

Baker and Blacksmith, pre-1900 This photograph, taken just before 1900, in the short street from Harford Square to the bottom of High Street, shows the bakery on the left and the smithy on the right. Mr. Gover, the baker, looks over the wall to his small cart with which he delivered the bread. The blacksmith, Sylvester Gallop died in 1915 aged 46 and was succeeded by his son Percy. The smithy was in the area which is now part of the Co-op Stores.

Blacksmiths outside the smithy The two blacksmiths in 1916, brothers-in-law Ernest Taylor and Percy Gallop, wait outside the smithy to deal with the horse brought by Arthur Brimble from Elm Farm. It was quite usual at that time for a queue of horses to be waiting to be shod at 6 o'clock in the morning.

Blacksmith at the forge Walter Spear was an orphan who had the good fortune to be apprenticed to the local blacksmith. In due course he succeeded to the business, retiring in 1955. With a reduction in the work with horses he turned to more general smithery and made some beautiful gates for local houses, some of which went in the drive for scrap metal during the war.

The Wheelwrights Walton House stands well back from the road at the top of High Street and was the wheelwright's. This is Frederick King with eleven of his workers and the tools of their craft. He built the row of houses down to and including the shop which is still run by his great grandson, David Walker, and his wife, Sheila.

Farming – Scything Through the ages this has been predominantly a farming area and all the old techniques were practised here. Haymaking started with the cutting of a swathe round the field and this is farmer Wallington Brimble making the first cut, in about 1900.

Farming – Mowing Then the heavy equipment moved in. After the horse-drawn mowing machine the next step was to turn the hay with a hand rake until it was nearly dry, then to pile it up into haycocks to complete the process.

Farming – Shearing On the local mixed farms the backbreaking job of shearing had to be done in the late spring. Because the flocks of sheep were small on local farms it was not usual to employ outside labour for the job.

Farming – Threshing Threshing could be done in late autumn or winter and necessitated a visit by the threshing machine. That would arrive as part of a noisy procession, the traction engine pulling the huge threshing machine, to which would be attached the sleeping hut for the driver and his mate, and finally the water tank on wheels. The threshing always attracted a crowd of sightseers who enjoyed the noise and bustle, and brought their dogs to deal with the rats which ran for cover as the last layer of the corn ricks was removed.

Lifting mangolds Before cattle food came as bags of concentrate from the 'West Midland Farmers' mangolds were grown as fodder, a heavy crop to harvest and store. They were put through the grinder, mixed with hay chaff and barley or oat meal, and laced with molasses. This view is of Bridge Farm, at the eastern end of the village, with members of the Peters family.

UNDER THE LAKE

When the Chew Valley Lake reservoir was made in the early 1950s almost twenty farms, homes and mills were demolished. Some of these were centuries old; a few were imposing buildings. A little information about four of them is included here to indicate the extent of the loss incurred in creating what is, without doubt, a great asset.

Whalley Court Much of the building was of 17th century construction and this view shows that older part immediately before it was demolished. An effigy of a lady with an anchor in her right hand, visible above the back door, was saved and is now in the porch of the Chew Stoke church. Tradition has it that Queen Elizabeth the First gave one of these to each of her naval commanders, one of whom was a Gilbert living here.
The last farmers were Edmund and Fred Keel whose ancestors had been tenants for over a century.

Whalley Court, the Georgian wing This drawing of the other side of the house shows how different was the architecture of the front and back. It was executed by S. Loxton in the 1920s.

Moreton Farm Joseph Leech, in his *Rural Rides* written a century ago, described the kitchen here, where sat Old Jenny and her spouse reading the family bible. The last farmer was George Curry, famous for his home-made cider. Very near was the base of Moreton Cross, which was removed to the Chew Stoke churchyard.

Spring Farm One of the most interesting farmsteads to be demolished, it was built in the early 17th century and still had its rough-hewn timber roof, large ingle-nook fireplace and a nail-studded front door. Adjoining was the Great Barn, 67 feet by 33 feet, and 35 feet high. The farm was bought by Maurice Hasell's father in 1940.

Stratford Mill This mill was in the parish of West Harptree and was producing flour as late as 1945. It was operated by an undershot wheel of 14 feet diameter. In 1950 Bristol Waterworks Company gave the mill to Bristol Corporation and it was carefully demolished and re-erected in the grounds of Blaize Castle. It is sometimes open to the public.

BISHOP SUTTON

Bishop Sutton Colliery (New Pit) 1922 This was one of several mines in the Bishop Sutton area and coal was produced from it intermittently from about 1835 to 1929. It was never very profitable because of thin seams and faults. The highest number employed was about 150 men and boys in 1921, with production up to 10,000 tons per annum, but it never recovered from the strikes of 1921 and 1926. The Lovells were the owners in its heyday. The head frame over the winding shaft is on the left of the picture and on the right is the house for the Cornish beam pump and the pumping shaft.

Bishop Sutton Colliery Rescue Brigade 1917 This squad was part of the North Somerset Rescue Organisation based at Midsomer Norton, where the equipment was kept until an emergency arose. The men were volunteers, unpaid for this duty and training in their spare time. Names of the team were, back row, G.G. Phillips (Instructor), J. Lovell (Colliery Owner), E. Reynolds (Leader), T.E. Moody (Manager), T. Sheppard and C.B. Blacker (Assistant Manager) and, in the front row, J. Harris and W. Tibbs.

Jesse Lovell, Entrepreneur Jesse Lovell was self-made. As a boy he worked in the Mendip mines and in 1867, when 20 years old, he came to Bishop Sutton and started trading, walking from one local village to another hawking tea. He soon had a pony and trap, then bought the shop in the village. He ended up owning a farm and a butchery, a wholesale drapery, the local coal mines, scores of cottages and a flour mill. He was a Methodist and had a large family, six sons and six daughters. He died in 1940, aged 93. The photograph shows Jesse with four of his sons.

Lovell's Mill This was the flour mill, situated across the road from the present-day Post Office. Most of it remains, converted into flats, but the part nearer to the road was demolished to allow for road widening.

CHEW STOKE

The Chew Stoke Inn in 1843 This is how W.W. Wheatley saw the inn, and it was much more picturesque than the present building. In a view of the interior drawn at the same time he shows the large ingle-nook fireplace round which the customers would sit.

Old Rectory Chew Stoke

The Old Rectory c.1905 This has returned to favour and is again The Rectory. The front door and the roof suggest that it is a 15th or very early 16th century building, but much altered at various times. This photograph shows the octagonal turret added late last century and now removed again. Rutter in 1829 said this was the Poor House of the village. Drawings of that time show some of the numerous coats of arms in different positions on this wall, also a door where the second window from the right is now, and no castellation on the eaves. So much of this wall has been rebuilt. Nevertheless it is a most interesting old building.

Cottages at Bottom Cross c.1916 These now make up the house adjoining the shop. There were four cottages here, two built in 1745 and the two further to the right in 1840. The property was owned by one family, in 1916 the Evans, and the people in the picture were, left to right, Miss Baker, Mrs. Hilda Dayman, Bert Dayman (in uniform), Charles Weeks, Mrs. Bessie Evans, unknown lady, and Wallington Evans in the trap. The building on the extreme right was the village bakery early this century and later it was the surgery for the school dentist and the office of the Registrar for Births and Deaths. The cottage just visible on the left was demolished in 1926 after a fire.

Brain's Garage c.1930 Norman Brain opened his garage in 1929 and, as well as repairing cars, motor cycles and bicycles, he had several side lines – cars for hire, selling radios and the batteries and accumulators they required. This gave rise to a service of regular recharging of the accumulators and a collection and delivery service to most local villages.

PENSFORD

The High Street c.1900 This was the original main road out of the village to the south. Even after the new road was made, about 1830, the stage coaches from Bristol to Wells and Weymouth would call at the two coaching inns in the village, the George and Dragon seen here on the left and the Rising Sun in Church Street. High Street was the site for the fairs held on 4th May and 8th November, when hurdle pens were erected for the sheep, and a wide variety of agricultural and domestic goods were sold from stalls. The tall house on the left, which has sometimes been called Viaduct View, is a rare example of a cruck type construction.

Lower High Street and the Lock-up It is said that early this century there were five shops in this short street, satisfying practically all the needs of the local people. The Round House or Lock-up, seen in the distance, was built about 1785 and was available as secure accommodation for anyone who had been arrested and was waiting to be taken before the magistrates. The last prisoner seems to have been a fourteen year old boy who was accused of stealing mangolds in 1895. Under the domed roof there is an octagonal building with two small openings through which food could be passed to the prisoner.

STATION ROAD, PENSFORD. 4.69.

The Bottom of Pensford Hill c.1904 This view shows, on the left, the Tabernacle and other buildings which have gone, and Tom Baber, the postman. On the right is the house, later a shop, in which Mrs. Barnes was burned to death, perhaps because she kept her stock of paraffin in an open bath. The vehicle is Primrose's delivery van and in the centre distance is the Rising Sun.

The Church and Bridge House The church of St. Thomas à Becket stands on an island between the River Chew and the mill stream. The tower is 14th century but the church was rebuilt in 1869. It was closed for worship in 1968, after the flood, and for a few years became the Becket Centre, a facility for exhibitions and meetings. Because of structural deterioration its future is now uncertain. Bridge House, on the left, consists of four sections built at different times. The earliest room was built about 1500 and was probably the Church Ale House, where the churchwardens would brew ale and sell it for the benefit of church maintenance or extension.

The last passenger train over the viaduct This was the 9.25 a.m. from Frome to Bristol on Saturday the 31st October 1959. After that there were goods trains only (mainly bringing coal from Radstock) and very occasional excursion trains, until closure of the line in 1968. Construction started in 1863 and the most expensive section was the Pensford viaduct, with sixteen arches, 995 feet in length and a maximum height to rail level of 95 feet. The viaduct is a listed structure and must be kept in repair by the British Railway Board although it will never again be crossed by trains.

Pensford Colliery c.1950 Otherwise known as Broadoak Pit. Sinking of the shafts commenced in 1910 but there were such problems that regular winding of coal was not possible until 1917. Normal production was about thirty waggons of coal a day but operation was rarely profitable because of the narrow seams and frequent faults. However, in 1955 it was the second largest mine in Somerset. It had its own washing plant for the small coal and pithead baths for the men. Three years later the National Coal Board decided it was uneconomic and closed it, making 328 men redundant.

The Broken Bridge Torrential rain (measured at Chew Stoke it was 6.8 inches in 6½ hours) caused much damage in Bristol and North Somerset on the 10th July 1968. A 'wall of water' rushed down the river and destroyed the new bridge but only removed the parapet of the older one, built about 1652, seen on the right. To bridge the 50 feet gap on this major road link the army moved in quickly and built a Bailey Bridge in only a few days.

Pensford Salvation Army Band The band was in great demand at functions and is here shown in about 1905 under the batton of Mr. Albert Gallop of Chew Magna, the serpent player. Note his violin and concertina in front of the drum. His brother Frank is on the extreme right and William Bailey is to the left of Albert.

STANTON DREW

Stanton Drew Mill 1883 A mill in Stanton Drew was recorded in the Domesday Survey of 1086 and it was probably on this site. It was owned by the Bishop of Bath and Wells from 1292 to the middle of the nineteenth century and it has been a corn mill (until 1499), a fulling mill (where new cloth was beaten to compact and soften it, until 1781), and a log-wood mill (making dye materials for use in cotton and wool mills). After a fire in 1863 it was rebuilt in 1874 by John Mardon, forerunner of Messrs. Mardon, Son and Hall of Bristol, and used to prepare salvaged material for use in making paper. It was bought and closed by Bristol Water Works Company in 1883 when they wished to reduce the flow in the River Chew to make more water available for Bristol. It became a private residence in the 1970s.

Bye Mills 1883 Joan Day, F.S.A. says at one time Bye Mills produced iron plate, but by 1714 it was a copper mill. The water-powered hammers continued in operation here until 1859 when the mill was bought by John Mardon, owner of the other mill, and he converted this one to paper production. It was closed in 1883 when Bristol Waterworks Company, wishing to take more water for Bristol and so reduce the flow of water in the River Chew, bought many of the mills along its course and closed them down. This photograph shows the mill in full production, with the workers' houses, a former copper mill building in the centre, stacks of barrels and sacks containing paper-making materials and, to the right of the bridge, the later paper-making building with its distinctive chimney.

Rectory Farm This house was earlier called The Parsonage or Parsonage Farm and was probably built for the Archdeacon of Bath in the mid-fifteenth century by Thomas Beckington, Bishop of Bath and Wells. That would account for his arms on the front of the house. Later the Coates family were tenants and, after 1821, William Wyllys, a sugar planter from Jamaica. He bought the estate and built Morley House next door, which was renamed Twyford House, then Mill Place.

The Manor House Now called Stanton Court and converted into a nursing home, this Georgian house replaced an earlier manor house which may have been fortified and was associated with a succession of important local families, the de Stantons, the Chokes, the Daubeneys, the Coopers and the Coates. The latter were in residence from early in the 18th century until 1920.

High Street and Druids' Arms This row of 18th century cottages contains the Druids' Arms, and the board gives M.A. Johnson as the name of the innkeeper. Kelly's Directory shows him in residence in 1902. An earlier tenant in 1848 was a Miss Lyde of the family whose coat of arms (a two-headed eagle) is often to be found locally. Just visible behind the lady on the right is the well, with its winding gear under a canopy. The present village hall, built as a lecture room in 1877 on land given by Mr. Coates, is visible on the left.

The Toll House This building was erected by the West Harptree Turnpike Trust soon after 1793 to house the toll keeper. Some of his equipment still exists, e.g. a desk under the window in the downstairs room and the bracket on the front of the house. This used to hold a leather pouch to receive the toll charge from drivers on high vehicles. The Trust was abolished in 1876 and the house has since been a unique residence and the subject of many photographs. This one shows the winding lane which ran from Chew Magna to Pensford.

114

The Toll House Keepers This couple may have been the Thomas Burridge (coachman) and his wife Ann (collector) who are shown in the census returns as living here in 1851 and 1871. Some quite large families have lived in the Round House, including the Pennys with their seven children early this century. This picture shows very clearly the leather pouch on its hinged bracket.

Church Farm This building shows three distinct stages of building and the earliest, of the 14th or 15th century, includes a two-storey hall with walls up to 36 inches thick. It had windows like those shown in the drawing at both ends of the hall but only the upper one of these two has survived. It was probably the church ale house of the village but another suggestion is that this may have been the fortified farm house which we know the St. Lo family had in the village.

Stanton Wick Glass Works This drawing in the Braikenridge Collection is labelled 'Brick Kiln near Stanton Drew' but it is almost certainly of the glass works at Stanton Wick. All that now remains of that is a mound in the field near the Carpenter's Arms, patches of dark soil and pieces of glass littering the ground. The works existed from the late 17th century until 1818, when fifteen local families of workers were transferred to Nailsea to work at the parent company there.

WEST HARPTREE

Gournay Court There were two manors of West Harptree and the family of de Gournay owned this one from soon after the Norman conquest. A Thomas de Gournay was involved in the murder of King Edward II at Berkeley Castle and later the estate reverted to the Crown. This house, with its fine Elizabethan-Jacobean frontage, was completed about 1650 by John Buckland, then leasing the manor. During the 1914–18 war it was a military hospital. The mansion was Duchy of Cornwall property and it was prepared as a home for Prince John, youngest son of King George V, but he died in 1919 before taking up residence. The house returned to private ownership in 1928. This drawing was done by John Buckler in 1835.

Gournay Court as a Military Hospital 1914–1918 The initiative in setting up this V.A.D. wartime convalescent hospital came from Lady Waldegrave, head of the Somerset Red Cross, and Dr. Shaw of Chew Magna. Many local people helped on the staff and among the names were Mr. and Mrs. C.W. Caples and Mr. J. Atkins of West Harptree and Miss. A. Chick, Miss F.G. Collins, Miss E.V. Viner-Johnson, Miss M.L. Wood, Mrs. Colston and Miss Shepperd of Chew Magna. A Wells photographer, Bert Phillips, visited weekly and took nearly six hundred photographs, mostly of groups and sometimes pretending to portray amusing situations. This one is supposed to be a reception committee welcoming the doctor.

West Harptree Village Centre c.1890 The shop was then owned by Collins, Draper and Grocer. At least some of the cottages on the right seem to be empty and derelict. They then had a small area in front fenced off from the road. The inn is thatched and the patient horses provide a marked contrast to the parked (and moving) cars of today.

Payne's Shop Ernest Payne acquired this shop about 1915 and after his death his son Vernon (here seen in the shop doorway) developed it as the centre of a small business empire with shops at Chew Stoke, Felton, Wells and Weston (Bath). The shop windows show a wide range of goods. Hidden behind the van was the large door to the warehouse.

Early Haulage Contractors Robert Horler and Albert Watts were brothers-in-law and business partners, involved in the making of Blagdon Lake and later in road making. A regular job was the hauling of used grain from the brewery at Oakhill to the farms, to be used as cattle feed. Kelly's Directory shows them in business from 1902.

The Hancock and Payne Fleet Tom Hancock was in the haulage business in the 1920s and later he joined up with Ernest Payne. They had about seven large vehicles, which included two steam lorries, shown in this photograph. Important fields of activity were the hauling of animal feeds from the Avonmouth docks and the delivery of coal. This photograph is taken in front of the Crown Inn. Drivers for the firm included William Stokes, Ted Durie, Dennis and Maurice Chapman, Mr. Branch and Percy Walford.

WINFORD

High Street c.1920 This was before the street was widened by taking in some of the gardens and before the surface was raised. The present trees are replacements of those in the photograph. The shop on the right (now Kingstone House) was a general store and Post Office, owned by Mrs. Croker (later Mrs. Haskins) and then by her neice, Mrs. Woofe. Mrs. Hawkins and her daughter Lillian are shown at the shop door, Tom Drake the postman holds his bicycle and Harry Ball, the village blacksmith and grandfather of Monty Ball, is driving the pony and trap. The Norton motorcycle and sidecar belonged to Bill Dyer. The white house in the background was thatched. It has since been reduced in size and has lost its front garden.

The Miners Arms Situated just below the road junction of Regil Lane and the Chew Magna road, this is now a private house, but it was the working men's pub in the village while the Prince of Waterloo was more up market. Albert George Bull is shown as the licensee but the photograph shows a later owner, Sydney Andow standing next to his wife (in white) and their child Betty. After his wife died Sydney never again opened for business and the premises remained unchanged until he died. The building is now much changed in appearance. The contents of the carts are a mystery. The small one seems to contain old boots and an iron bedstead, perhaps belonging to a rag and bone merchant.

Harvest Home: The Worle Gate c.1898 The manager of the red ochre mines near Regil, the Reddings, was Richard Cattle. He married Mary Worle, widow of P.C. Worle, and she had four children, of whom the eldest, Walter, followed his stepfather as Manager. His family, the Worles, are associated with a tradition that for the Harvest Home each September they created a decorative arch made of vegetables and flowers, built between the Prince of Waterloo and the stream. Walter and his wife Alice are in the centre of the arch and probably the rest are members of the family.

Miss Lovell at Kentshares Farm Farmer Lovell had three unmarried daughters living at home and this is one of them in front of the farmhouse. The sisters ran a private school here from the beginning of the century until about 1930 which was well supported by children from the nearby villages. In appearance the house has changed scarcely at all.

Winford Iron Ore Co. Traction Engine George Pickford, who was engineer at the Reddings, recognises this as 'Progress I', the first traction engine owned by the company. Until replaced about 1920, it was used to take the iron ore from the works at Littleton, where it had been ground to powder, to the factory at Malago for the further treatment which produced a red dye. That was used by Marley Tiles in their tiles and lino, for paint and for marking sheep. Some was taken straight to the docks in Bristol. Often an engine like this pulled two trailers, a serious obstacle in our narrow country lanes and very destructive of the road surface.

School Group c.1924 This was the class of Ernest Elworthy, Headmaster from 1886 to 1924. He was only 23 when he succeeded his father, James Elworthy, and father and son taught consecutively for 75 years in the village school. He died in 1942, aged 79 years, after a life of public service, having been a magistrate, Chairman of the Parish Council, Clerk to the Charity Trustees, and a devoted church worker as organist, churchwarden, preacher and bell ringer.

Winford Market The cattle market was started before the First World War behind the Prince of Waterloo, with William King as the first autioneer, to be followed by his son Edgar. The market moved to the site between Barrow Lane and Felton Lane, as shown here. Mr. Edgar King is on the extreme right, with his back to the camera, and many others can be recognised, including Jim Stevens of Blagdon (now over 90 years of age). The market dealt in cattle (beef and milk), calves, pigs, sheep, chickens and eggs, and rabbits. In 1974 the market moved to its present site outside the village and the old site became a housing estate. The King connection ended in 1989 when Jim King ceased to be the auctioneer.

Tug-of-war Team There was strong competition between the tug-of-war teams from the local villages, with leagues and cups to be won. This was Winford's second team in 1933 and Jim Cole, then about 17 years old, remembers being pressed into service because of the illness of a regular member. Names of participants were, back row, Tom Vowles (trainer), Ernest Ogborne, George Harrison, Jim Cole, Wilfred Hall and Fred Blackmore (coach); front row, Henry Harrison, Chappie Cole, Sunny Cole and Harold Wyatt.

Winford Voluntary Services 1939–45 The organisations represented in this group include the Special Constables, Air Raid Wardens, the Women's Voluntary Service, the Fire Brigade, St. John's Ambulance Brigade and the Girls' Training Corps.